Novels for Students, Volume 18

Project Editor: David Galens

Editorial: Anne Marie Hacht, Ira Mark Milne, Pam Revitzer, Kathy Sauer, Timothy J. Sisler, Jennifer Smith, Carol Ullmann, Maikue Vang Research: Nicodemus Ford, Sarah Genik, Tamara Nott Permissions: Shalice Shah-Caldwell

Manufacturing: Stacy Melson

Imaging and Multimedia: Dean Dauphinais, Leitha Etheridge-Sims, Mary Grimes, Lezlie Light, Luke Rademacher Product Design: Pamela A. E. Galbreath, Michael Logusz © 2003 by Gale. Gale is an imprint of The Gale group, Inc., a division of Cengage Learning Inc.

For more information, contact

The Gale Group, Inc.

27500 Drake Rd.

Farmington Hills, MI 48331–3535

service, or individual does not imply endorsement of the editors or publisher. Errors brought to the attention of the publisher and verified to the satisfaction of the publisher will be corrected in future editions.

ISBN 0-7876-6030-2
ISSN 1094-3552

Printed in the United States of America
10 9 8 7 6 5 4 3 2 1

The Unbearable Lightness of Being

Milan Kundera

1984

Introduction

First published in 1984 in both Paris and New York, Milan Kundera's *The Unbearable Lightness of Being* is a rich and complicated novel that is at once a love story, a metaphysical treatise, a political commentary, a psychological study, a lesson on kitsch, a musical composition in words, an aesthetic exploration, and a meditation on human existence. As an expatriate Czechoslovakian writer, Kundera draws upon his firsthand experience of the 1968

Prague Spring and subsequent Soviet occupation of his country to provide the backdrop for the story of four people whose lives are inextricably enmeshed. Because the work is so complex, there are many themes that intertwine throughout the novel, just as a theme in a musical composition will be introduced only to reappear later in a different key. Indeed there are several critics who focus their entire analysis on the way Kundera uses musical structure to put together his novel. At its most fundamental level, *The Unbearable Lightness of Being* is about the ambiguity and paradoxes of human existence, as each person teeters between lightness and weight; between the belief that all is eternal return and Nietzsche's concept that life is an ever-disappearing phenomenon; and between dream and reality.

Author Biography

Milan Kundera was born April 1, 1929, in Brno, Czechoslovakia (now the Czech Republic), the son of Ludvik and Milada Kundera. He studied music with Paul Haas and Vaclav Kapral and attended Charles University in Prague. He studied film at the Academy of Music and Dramatic Arts in Prague, where he later held a position as assistant professor from 1958 to 1969. He was a member of the central committee of the Czechoslovak Writers Union from 1963 to 1969.

In 1962 Kundera began writing his first novel, *The Joke*. The book caused problems with the national censors, and consequently it was not published until 1967 (the English edition was first published in 1969). Kundera's frustration with the censors climaxed with a speech he gave at the Fourth Czechoslovak Writers Congress. However, Kundera and others who followed his lead were subjected to even more oppression.

For a brief period in 1968 known as the "Prague Spring," the government eased restrictions on its writers and citizens. The Soviet Bloc countries, led by the Soviet Union, were nervous about the relaxation of the regime in Czechoslovakia, and in August 1968, Russian tanks and Soviet Bloc soldiers took control of Prague. The Soviets deposed Czech leader Alexander Dubcek and put Gustav Husak in his place, instituting a repressive regime that lasted for twenty-one years. During this time, Kundera's books and plays were banned, and his works could not be sold in bookstores or read in libraries. Kundera was forbidden to publish in Czechoslovakia, and he lost his teaching position.

In 1975 Kundera received permission to immigrate to France, where he became a professor. His 1979 novel *The Book of Laughter and Forgetting* (first published in English in 1980) led the Czech government to revoke his citizenship. In 1981 Kundera became a French citizen.

Although by 1984 Kundera was internationally respected as a writer, his novel *The Unbearable Lightness of Being* secured his place in world literature. Since that time, Kundera has published widely, including the novels *Immortality*, published in French in 1990 and English in 1991; *Slowness: A Novel*, published in French in 1995, and English in 1996; *Identity: A Novel*, published in French in 1997 and in English in 1998; and *Ignorance*, published in English in 2002. Kundera's work has been well-received by critics and readers alike, and he has been awarded many prizes, including the Czechoslovak Writers Union prize in 1968 for *The Joke*; the Commonwealth Award for distinguished service in literature in 1981; a 1984 *Los Angeles Times* Book Prize for *The Unbearable Lightness of Being*; and the Academie Francaise critics prize in 1987.

Part 1: Lightness and Weight

The novel opens with a meditation on philosopher Friedrich Nietzsche's idea of the eternal return, contrasted with the notion of *einmal ist keinmal*; that is, "what happens but once ... might as well not have happened at all." According to Nietzsche, eternal return is the "heaviest of burdens." The absence of this burden, however, renders life inconsequential. The binary opposition of weight and lightness continues throughout the book.

Kundera next introduces Tomas, a surgeon who has fallen in love with a young woman named Tereza. Tomas has many mistresses, engaging in what he terms "erotic friendships." When Tereza discovers Tomas's many mistresses, she is distraught. It is this contrast between the weight of Tereza's love and the lightness of Tomas's love that provides much of the material for the book.

Eventually Tomas marries Tereza. He also buys Tereza a puppy they name Karenin. Although married, Tomas does not give up his mistresses. Notable among them is Sabina, an artist. Sabina clearly understands Tomas and even becomes a close friend of Tereza's.

In 1968 the Russian occupation of

Czechoslovakia begins. Sabina immigrates to Switzerland, and Tomas begins receiving calls from a Swiss doctor who wants him to immigrate to Switzerland as well. Tomas and Tereza do well in Zurich for six or seven months, until Tereza learns that Tomas is once again seeing Sabina. Tereza returns to Prague, and within days Tomas follows her.

Part 2: Soul and Body

The story returns to the beginning, this time from Tereza's point of view. This section allows the reader to understand the family background and psychology that drive Tereza. Her father was a political prisoner who died in jail, and her mother is an abusive, vulgar woman who takes great delight in humiliating Tereza. Kundera reiterates Tereza's meeting with Tomas and her decision to go to Prague. Also in this section the reader learns of Tereza's troubling dreams, which often involve Tomas. Finally, the friendship between Sabina and Tereza grows; it is Sabina who has secured a position for Tereza at the magazine where Sabina works. In one particularly intense scene, Sabina and Tereza photograph each other nude at Sabina's studio.

Part 3: Words Misunderstood

In this section the reader meets Franz, a university professor in Geneva who is having an affair with Sabina. Franz is married to a woman named Marie-Claude, whom he does not love. Throughout this section, there are brief chapters of "misunderstood words" that illustrate the differences between Sabina and Franz. For example, in a section titled "Music," Franz tries to explain his love of music to Sabina. Kundera writes, "For Franz music was the art that comes closest to Dionysian beauty in the sense of intoxication." For Sabina, however, music is noise. Her early years at the Academy of Arts ruined her feelings for music, as the school played loud, cheerful music on speakers from early morning until night. While for Franz music is a liberating force, for Sabina music is an unpleasant reminder of her life in the totalitarian state. Likewise, in a short section titled "Light and Dark," the reader discovers that Franz is drawn to darkness and that he closes his eyes when he makes love to Sabina. For Sabina, however, "living … meant seeing."

Given the distance between the two lovers in their understanding of reality, it is not surprising that Franz chooses to tell his wife of their affair, the very thing Sabina does not want to happen. Consequently, Sabina leaves Franz and Switzerland, settling first in Paris and later in the United States. She receives a letter while in Paris from Tomas's son, informing her that Tomas and Tereza have been killed in a car accident. Franz becomes involved with a student and begins taking an active role in political dissension.

Media Adaptations

- *The Unbearable Lightness of Being* was adapted as a film in 1988. The film was directed by Phillip Kaufman, and stars Daniel Day-Lewis and Juliette Binoche. The film is available on DVD from Home Vision Entertainment.

- *The Unbearable Lightness of Being* was recorded on audiocassette in 1988 by Books on Tape (Newport Beach, CA). Christopher Hurt is the reader.

Part 4: Body and Soul

Tomas is working as a window washer in this section, having lost his position at the hospital.

Tereza tends bar. Their schedules are very different from each other, and, by the time Tereza returns home from work each night, Tomas is asleep. When she crawls into bed beside him, she is aware of an odor coming from his hair, an odor she finally identifies as coming from the genitals of another woman. This weighs heavily on her, and she eventually has a sexual encounter with an engineer she meets at the bar. Only later does she realize that the engineer is probably a spy for the state. The atmosphere of this section is sad and heavy throughout, and the pressure of living in a totalitarian state, where there is little or no privacy, permeates the events. Perhaps the most moving part of this section is a dream Tereza has in which Tomas instructs her to go up Petrin Hill, which she does, only to find men with rifles killing those who want to die. It must be their choice, the men tell Tereza. At the last minute she says that being killed is not her choice. Although this is how the dream ends, it seems that Tereza truly does want to die.

Part 5: Lightness and Weight

In this section, the reader discovers why Tomas has been let go from his job at the hospital. It seems that he wrote a letter to an editor of a journal during the brief Prague Spring. Now, with the reinstatement of a more oppressive regime, he is called upon to recant. He refuses to do so and must consequently resign from his job. His friends and family think he is protesting the new regime. Thus, he is approached by his son Simon and the editor of the journal who published his letter. They want him to sign a petition demanding the release of Czech political prisoners. He refuses to sign this document. Finally, to get away from the intrigue and anxieties of the city, Tomas and Tereza move to a collective farm in the country, believing that this move will put them so far down on the social ladder that the state will no longer be concerned with them, since they have little else to lose.

Part 6: The Grand March

In this section Kundera explores the notion of kitsch, particularly communist kitsch. The story also returns to Franz, who decides to go to Thailand with a group of intellectuals to protest human-rights violations in Cambodia. While there, he is senselessly mugged by some street thugs and ends up dying in a hospital shortly after his return to Switzerland.

Part 7: Karenin's Smile

In this final section, the reader learns more about Tomas and Tereza's life on the farm. Their dog Karenin is very old and dying of cancer. This death affects both of them deeply. At the collective, Tomas has finally given up womanizing, and Tereza asks for forgiveness for her role in his unhappiness in life. Tomas replies that he has been happy these last years at the farm. Thus in the hours before their deaths, Tomas and Tereza are happy together.

Characters

Franz

Franz is a professor who lives in Geneva, Switzerland. He enters the book in the third part, where he is introduced as Sabina's lover of nine months. Franz is married to Marie-Claude, a woman he does not love but whom he married because she loved him so much. He also has a daughter, Marie-Anne, who is the carbon copy of her mother. For twenty-three years, Franz has been a loyal, if unhappy, husband. Now, however, he finds he is in love with Sabina. Throughout the months of their affair, he has taken trouble to separate his lover and his wife, refusing to make love to Sabina in Geneva, choosing rather to take her on trips all over the world. He is constantly unsure of Sabina, however, and always seems to expect she will leave him. As the narrator informs the reader, for Franz love "meant a longing to put himself at the mercy of his partner....love meant the constant expectation of a blow."

Thus, although Franz is a physically strong man, he is an emotionally weak man. He places no demands on Sabina, nor does he use his strength against her. Instead he chooses to be weak. Sabina does not find this quality attractive.

A turning point in Franz's life occurs when his wife holds a gallery opening and invites Sabina, whose pictures have been shown in her gallery. When Marie-Claude insults Sabina by telling her that her pendant is ugly, Franz decides he must tell Marie-Claude about the affair in order to protect Sabina. The situation backfires: Marie-Claude throws Franz out of the house but will not grant him a divorce, and Sabina leaves him.

This turn of events underscores a fundamental quality in Franz, namely his inability to understand women—particularly Sabina. The chapters of the book that involve Franz and Sabina are written like a dictionary, with definitions of "misunderstood words." Ultimately, it becomes clear that Franz is more in love with the idea of Sabina than with Sabina herself, and, thus, her physical absence is less of a problem than one might expect. Throughout the rest of his life, Franz always imagines Sabina is watching him, although he never sees her again.

In the sixth part of the book, Franz decides to join a group of Western intellectuals who travel to Thailand to protest Cambodian human rights violations. In an utterly senseless act, he is killed by muggers in the streets of Thailand, yet another indication of Franz's fundamental misunderstanding of humankind and reality. The final irony is that "in death, Franz at last belonged to his wife....Marie-Claude took care of everything: she saw to the funeral, sent out the announcements, bought the wreaths, and had a black dress made—a wedding dress, in reality. Yes, a husband's funeral is a wife's true wedding! The climax of her life's work! The reward for her suffering!" Franz's death serves to underscore the futility of his life.

Sabina

Sabina is a Czech painter and one of Tomas's many lovers. The product of the Communist system of education, she is an artist who detests kitsch, noise, social realism, and music. It is through Sabina that Kundera comments on the influence of politics on art and music, as well as on the life of the political exile.

Ironically, Sabina is the character that has relationships with all of the other characters, although she is by far the most distant and distancing of all the characters. Her affair with Tomas in Prague is a good representation of the kind of relationship she desires, one of sex and friendship without emotional commitment. When Sabina and Tomas meet in Switzerland to make love, it is their last such encounter. She wears nothing but her lingerie and a bowler hat that belonged to her grandfather, someone she never actually knew. The scene is both emotionally and sexually charged and clearly touches Sabina emotionally in a place where she does not want to be touched.

Likewise, Sabina enjoys being with Franz so long as there is little commitment. As soon as Franz tells his wife he is having an affair with Sabina, Sabina disappears from Franz's life. However, it is Sabina's scene with Tereza which is perhaps the most sexually and emotionally charged scene of the book. Tereza comes to take photographs of Sabina in her studio and suggests that she photograph Sabina nude. Sabina, for all her sexual libertinism, cannot comply immediately. Rather, Sabina first drinks three glasses of wine and talks about her grandfather's bowler hat. It is not until Tereza distances herself by picking up her camera and looking through the lens that Sabina throws open her robe. After both women take pictures of each other and find themselves enchanted by the situation, Sabina "almost frightened by the enchantment and eager to dispel it ... burst[s] into loud laughter." Clearly the situation with Tereza is fraught with emotional content, something Sabina will not allow herself to feel.

Tereza

Tereza is a young woman from a small village who, through a whole series of coincidences, becomes Tomas's lover and later his wife. Tereza's father was a political prisoner who died in jail, leaving Tereza in the care of her vulgar, loud mother, who took great delight in embarrassing Tereza. This abuse led to Tereza's radical split between body and soul; as much as possible she rejects everything about her body. It is her soul she gives to Tomas, and thus she represents heaviness in the burden of love she places on Tomas.

Tereza loves Tomas ferociously and, although she cannot tolerate his philandering, she cannot leave him. It seems as if her role in the book is to bear suffering. Her dreams are particularly painful. In one, she must parade nude around a swimming pool with other nude women. Tomas sits on a high chair and shoots any woman who does not perform proper knee bends. Later in the book, Tereza dreams that Tomas takes her to Petrin Hill, where he has arranged for men with guns to shoot her if she so chooses. When Tereza shares these dreams with Tomas, he finds himself ever more deeply enmeshed with his wife. Although through much of the book the two of them make each other unhappy, they nonetheless are unable to part from each other.

A turning point comes for Tereza when she returns home from work one night and smells another woman on her sleeping husband. In an act of rebellion, she ends up having a one-time sexual encounter with an engineer. Later she comes to believe this engineer is really a member of the secret police sent to entrap her for prostitution. After this event, Tereza tries to persuade Tomas to move to a collective farm in the country. When Tomas asks Tereza what has been bothering her these past months, she tells him of the odor his hair has been emitting. This revelation is enough to convince Tomas they must move to the country. Tereza finally achieves what she wants—Tomas's fidelity.

Tomas

Tomas is a successful Czech surgeon who lives

in Prague. In addition to being a fine surgeon, Tomas is also an inveterate womanizer. He has many affairs and has constructed a set of rules for preventing these affairs from becoming anything other than occasions for sex.

While on a conference to a small town, he meets Tereza, a barmaid. He tells Tereza to look him up if she is ever in Prague, which she does. Tomas finds himself in love with Tereza when she comes down with influenza during her visit. However, he also finds these feelings "inexplicable." He ponders the question, is this love? Or, he wonders, "[Is] it simply the hysteria of a man who, aware deep down of his inaptitude for love, [feels] the self-deluding need to simulate it?" Tomas does not have the answer to this question, but nonetheless he feels drawn to marry Tereza. Marriage, however, does not stop Tomas from pursuing affairs with a variety of women.

For Tomas, sexual intercourse and love are not necessarily connected. He discovers this when he realizes how much he loves to sleep with Tereza, something he never does with his lovers. Tomas concludes, "Making love with a woman and sleeping with a woman are two separate passions, not merely different but opposite. Love does not make itself felt in the desire for copulation (a desire that extends to an infinite number of women) but in the desire for shared sleep (a desire limited to one woman)."

Tomas's career suffers after the Soviet occupation of Prague. When he is offered the opportunity of immigrating to Switzerland, he takes it. In Switzerland he takes up with one of his former lovers, Sabina, who has also immigrated there. However, after just a few months in Switzerland, Tereza leaves him to return to Prague. Tomas chooses to follow her after a few days, and, from the time of his return to Prague, his career goes downhill. In the repressive atmosphere of the new government, he loses his job and begins working as a window washer. Even as a window washer, however, he finds opportunities to make love to many women.

Tomas is, in many ways, an enigma. Although he loves Tereza with all his heart, he is unable to put an end to his philandering in spite of the pain it causes his wife. If he feels strongly the idea of *es muss sein* (it must be) applies to his relationship with his wife, he feels likewise about his relationship with other women. It is not until confronted with the odor emanating from his hair that he realizes he must give up all other women. He moves to the country with Tereza.

Of all the characters in the book, Tomas is the one who undergoes the most radical change from beginning to end. Just hours before his death, he dances with Tereza and tells her that he has been happy with her in the country, a happiness that seemed to have eluded him for much of his life.

Love and Sex

For all of its other concerns, *The Unbearable Lightness of Being* is first an exploration of the many facets of love. In his or her own way, each of the four main characters confronts and wrestles with the notion of love. Tomas, for example, never equates sex with love. Before Tereza comes into his life, he is very happy with his "erotic friend-ships." Because these affairs do not pretend to be "love" affairs, he is able to move among many women without betraying any of them. When Tereza arrives at his apartment and becomes ill, he realizes that he feels compassion for her, and that compassion itself is love. In spite of his many affairs, he does not leave Tereza, nor is there any doubt he loves her deeply.

For Tereza, however, love carries a very different connotation. While she does not equate love and sex, when she offers her body to Tomas, she does so out of love. Indeed for Tereza love is an offering of everything. That Tomas does not reciprocate in kind is a source of bitter sorrow to Tereza. Her love is of the "heavy" kind, a burden for both Tomas and Tereza herself.

Sabina, like Tomas, has many affairs and refuses to commit to one person. Of all the characters in the book, she is the one who seems least able to love and connect emotionally with another human being. Kundera is connecting her emotional damage to her upbringing within the Soviet system. As a child, Sabina found herself constantly under the barrage of the state, in the form of the music that was played all day at the Academy for Fine Arts; the parades in which the students were forced to march; and the strict aesthetic rules of social realism. To be an artist in Soviet-controlled Czechoslovakia required complete compliance with state doctrine. For an artist, it also required a complete dampening of the creative forces and emotional responses, creating an individual who is always wary of revealing what is under the surface.

Franz too is emotionally incompetent and unable to engage in a loving relationship, although he believes himself to be in love with Sabina. As the book continues, it becomes clear that Franz loves his idea of Sabina, not Sabina herself. Tellingly, Franz closes his eyes as he makes love to Sabina, effectively erasing the woman in bed with him and substituting his own idea of Sabina in her place. In addition, when Franz misguidedly chooses to tell his wife about his affair with Sabina, he demonstrates how poorly he knows either woman. His wife does not respond at all as he imagines she will. Even worse, Sabina leaves him. After Sabina's departure, Franz in many ways is happier than when she was present. Because his idea of Sabina is somehow stronger in her absence, Franz no longer needs to square his idea of Sabina with the physical reality of Sabina.

Politics and Government

The Unbearable Lightness of Being is a political novel. It not only describes politics within the Soviet bloc, it takes as its subject political and governmental oppression. None of the characters in the book can escape from the tentacles of totalitarianism that threaten to strangle each one. When Tomas, for example, during the brief Prague Spring writes an essay critical of the Communist Party, he opens himself to a series of damaging responses. After the Soviet invasion and the reinstitution of a repressive regime, Tomas is asked to recant his statement in order to keep his job as a surgeon. Tomas refuses, a stance that signals to his countrymen that he is a dissident himself. Tomas chooses to resign from the hospital and take a job as a window washer, thinking that in this way he can escape from governmental observation. However, when his son and the editor of the journal that published his essay ask him to sign a petition calling for the release of political prisoners, Tomas refuses. What both the government and the dissidents miss about Tomas is that he is largely apolitical; that is, he is someone who wants to carry on his life as a doctor without the intrusion of either government or politics. Such a stance is completely untenable, however. As a public figure, the government uses its strength to attack Tomas in the public sphere, by not allowing him to pursue the one thing at which he excels—practicing surgery.

In contrast, Tereza is a very private person, and the claustrophobia of totalitarianism affects her in a very private way. She finds herself working as a barmaid as the result of Tomas's published essay. The bar is both seedy and disreputable; even so, there are patrons who try to bring the power of the state down on Tereza. Most notably, when she has a brief affair with an engineer, she does not consider until later that, in all likelihood, the engineer is really a member of the secret police. For Tereza, the worst kind of governmental intrusion would be into her sexual life. She imagines that photographs have been taken of her with the engineer and that these pictures will later be used against her. Thus, for the private Tereza, the invasion of her personal space signifies the ultimate victory of the state over the person.

Topics For Further Study

- In part six of *The Unbearable Lightness of Being*, Kundera writes at length about the notion of "kitsch." Define kitsch. Find examples in magazines of kitsch from twenty-first-century American culture. Create a collage using these images that gives the viewer insight as to the role of kitsch in the United States.

- Reread the sections of *The Unbearable Lightness of Being* that describe Tereza's dreams. Read several entries on dreams from psychology textbooks or reference works. What do these books indicate that Tereza's dreams reveal about her?

- Research the literary history of Czechoslovakia in the twentieth century. Who are some notable writers and their subjects? Create a timeline to locate these writers historically and to connect them with important events of their time. On your timeline, be sure to include illustrations, note major works, and identify important historical events.

- Define social realism. Using art-history books, encyclopedias, and reference works, identify the underpinning principles of social realism. Write a report explaining what you have discovered. Use images you find on the World Wide

Web to illustrate your points.

- Research the lives of Alexander Dubcek and Vaclav Havel. What roles did these two important Czechs play in the history of their country?

Just as the state intrudes on Tomas's public work life and Tereza's private sex life, the state intrudes on Sabina in her most vulnerable area—her art. In response to the Soviet invasion, Sabina leaves Czechoslovakia. She has already experienced what the state can do to art and has no desire to experience it again. Ironically, the tentacles of the state follow her into exile. She finds herself uncomfortably lumped together with all exiled Czech intellectuals; her work receives notice and praise not for the work itself but for her status as a dissident. Even within the émigré community, she finds herself surrounded with politics that will destroy her by forcing her to conform to some ideal other than her own. As Sabina wanders farther and farther away from her homeland, the political situation she left behind continues to shape her.

Kitsch

Kundera spends considerable energy to define, describe, and investigate the role of kitsch in communist society. "Kitsch" is a German word that loosely means inferior, sentimental, and/or vulgar art. Although kitsch claims to have an aesthetic purpose, it tends to simplify complicated ideas and thoughts into stereotypical and easily marketable forms. Kitsch appeals to the masses and to the lowest common denominator. It is the world of greeting-card poetry and velvet Elvis. For kitsch to be kitsch, it must be able to evoke an emotional response that according to the book "the multitudes can share."

Kitsch then is essential for the emotional and intellectual control of a populace in a totalitarian culture. In a system that requires all people to feel the same way about a particular event or state of being, kitsch works its magic. As Kundera writes, "Those of us who live in a society where various political tendencies exist side by side and competing influences cancel or limit one another can manage more or less to escape the kitsch inquisition: the individual can preserve his individuality; the artists can create unusual works. But whenever a single political movement corners power, we find ourselves in the realm of *totalitarian kitsch*." Kitsch, according to Kundera, is devoid of irony, since "in the realm of kitsch everything must be taken quite seriously."

Understanding kitsch brings the reader to an understanding of Sabina: it is not communism that repels her; it is communist kitsch such as the May Day parades and the art of social realism. And those who criticize kitsch, or for that matter call it kitsch, must be banned for life because it is the expression of individualism that poses the greatest threat to the totalitarian regime. Kundera concludes, "In this light, we can regard the gulag as a septic tank used by totalitarian kitsch to dispose of its refuse."

Style

Narrator

One of the most interesting devices that Kundera uses in *The Unbearable Lightness of Being* is his creation of a narrator. When the book opens, the reader encounters a meditation on the ideas of German philosopher Friedrich Nietzsche and classical Greek philosopher Parmenides. What soon becomes clear is that there is a narrative voice undertaking this meditation, a voice that is creating and participating in the story while remaining somehow outside the story: "Not long ago, I caught myself experiencing a most incredible sensation. Leafing through a book on Hitler, I was touched by some of his portraits: they reminded me of my childhood. I grew up during the war; several members of my family perished in Hitler's concentration camps; but what were their deaths compared with the memories of a lost period in my life, a period that would never return?" Many readers will conclude the narrator is Kundera himself. Later in the story, the narrator tells the reader he has "been thinking about Tomas for many years," implying it is the author-as-narrator who has given Tomas his fictional existence. Likewise, the narrator tells the reader that Tereza began as a rumbling in his stomach.

However, while it may be easy to make the

assumption that the "I" in the story is Kundera, it also does not take much of a stretch to consider the narrator as yet another character in the story itself, somehow a part of Kundera yet also separate from him. This technique is not new; Geoffrey Chaucer uses it in *The Canterbury Tales*, the famous fourteenth-century classic, when he creates a persona for himself as one of the pilgrims.

Why would a writer do such a thing? Kundera's narrator serves the function of setting up the philosophical structure of the novel. Because he is separate from the story, he is able to comment on each of the characters outside the knowledge of the characters themselves. This distance allows the reader to share privileged knowledge with the narrator that is hidden from the characters. It also leads the reader to trust that the narrator is reliable.

A second reason Kundera may choose to create a narrator is as a device to continually remind the reader that what he or she is reading is fiction, not reality. Authorial intrusions such as those made by the narrator serve to place the story in the realm of fiction, while making the author seem more present to the reader. It seems that the author is speaking directly to the reader in a kind of conversation.

However, a closer examination of this second purpose complicates the role of the narrator even further. While it may *seem* that the author is engaging the reader in conversation, what is *really* happening is that the reader is looking at black marks on paper, black marks the writer set down a number of years ago. The words on the page, no matter how much they recall the spoken voice, remain carefully crafted traces of some human creator. When the reader is forced to confront the essential artificiality of fiction itself, the narrator out of necessity becomes a character himself. While the words revealing his thoughts about the characters and about human existence may indeed coincide with Kundera's own thoughts, once Kundera has chosen to write himself into the book, he has created a fictional persona who will tell the story as best he is able.

Setting

The Unbearable Lightness of Being is set during the 1960s in Czechoslovakia. The fact that Kundera himself experienced the Prague Spring as well as the Soviet takeover lends special poignancy to the story. Kundera uses his setting for several important purposes. *The Unbearable Lightness of Being* is a love story and juxtaposing the love affairs of the four main characters with the upheaval of the Russian invasion throws the issues of love into sharp contrast with the issues of hate. In addition, it is the setting that allows Kundera to use his novel as a vehicle for a consideration of the effects of the totalitarian regime on the creation of art and, by extension, on the creation of life itself.

Compare & Contrast

- **1960s:** Czechoslovakia is firmly part

of the Warsaw Pact, a military alliance that includes the Soviet Union and the Eastern Bloc countries.

Today: The Czech Republic has joined the North Atlantic Treaty Organization (NATO), a military alliance that includes the United States and western European Nations.

- **1960s:** Beginning in 1962, the Czechoslovakian government begins to make movements toward reform, easing the restrictions on its citizens. In 1968, during what is known as the Prague Spring, several writers and artists speak out against totalitarianism. Within months, Soviet tanks invade Czechoslovakia, and the country is forcibly brought back within Soviet domination. It is a time of great repression.

Today: The Czech Republic, after a period of economic reform, applies for membership in the European Union in 1996 and expects to be granted admission in 2004. At the same time, the country has maintained its close ties with some of the former Warsaw Pact nations. The Social Democratic party, under the leadership of Vladimir Spidla, wins the general election in June

2002.

- **1960s:** Writers and artists in Czechoslovakia are forced to submit their work to state-sponsored censors. All works are subjected to the aesthetic of "social realism." Works that do not conform are banned. Nevertheless, there is an active underground of writers and artists who continue to produce high quality work, although it cannot be published or shown in Czechoslovakia. Many writers and artists are forced to leave their homes and are subjected to severe oppression in their homeland.

  Today: Works by dissident Czech writers now circulate in Czechoslovakia. Vaclav Havel, himself a noted dissident writer who spent four years in prison under the old regime, is elected president of the Czech Republic in 1993. Many exiled Czech writers are able to return to their homeland for visits.

The History of Czechoslovakia

The land that became Czechoslovakia was actually separate regions within the Austro-Hungarian Empire until the end of World War I. The Czech people made their homes in Bohemia and Moravia, parts of Austria, while the Slovaks resided in Slovakia, part of Hungary. While quite different in their interests, concerns, and industrialization, after World War I the two regions declared independence as the Republic of Czechoslovakia. They were briefly democratic in the years between the two world wars; however, in 1938 Adolph Hitler invaded the new nation, occupying Prague.

After the defeat of the Germans, Czechoslovakia was reestablished; however, the Soviet Union exerted its influence on the young nation, and in 1948 the Communists seized power, establishing a government much like Joseph Stalin's in the Soviet Union. During the 1950s and early 1960s, the Communist Party ruled all areas of life, including the government, art, education, and culture.

The Prague Spring, 1968

In the 1960s, leaders such as Alexander

Dubcek attempted to introduce modest political reforms. In this atmosphere of lessening repression, writers and artists came forward and asked for even more reforms to be quickly undertaken. In June 1967 Kundera himself addressed the Fourth Czechoslovak Writers Congress and called for open discussion and an end to repression and censorship. Many who spoke up at this meeting were punished.

This punishment did not put a stop to the push for reform. In January 1968, Dubcek became secretary of the party and attempted to make Czechoslovakian socialism more humane. The movement did not sit well with the Warsaw Pact nations, particularly the Soviet Union, which did not want any of its satellite nations to shift their orbits significantly.

The Soviet Invasion, August 1968

Consequently, in August 1968, troops from the U.S.S.R. and other Eastern Bloc nations invaded Czechoslovakia. The occupation resulted in Dubcek's removal and the end of the reform movement. The Soviets instituted a new Czechoslovakian regime that was both harsh and repressive. Writers such as Kundera lost their jobs and were prohibited from speaking publicly or publishing their works. For some seven years, Kundera was not allowed to travel to the West.

Conditions in Czechoslovakia remained largely the same until 1989, in spite of the growing reform movement in the Soviet Union inspired by President

Mikhail Gorbachev. However, the fall of the Berlin Wall in 1989 opened the floodgates in Czechoslovakia as well. Ultimately, democracy was restored in Czechoslovakia but not without trouble. In the early 1990s, Slovakia, the eastern part of the country, wanted greater autonomy. Many Slovakians called for complete independence. At the same time, Czech nationalists also wanted their own country. Although President Havel strongly opposed the split, the people of the country voted in 1992 for candidates in favor of dividing the country. Consequently, in January 1993, Czechoslovakia became two independent nations, now known as the Czech Republic and Slovakia.

Critical Overview

When *The Unbearable Lightness of Being* appeared in 1984, it immediately became an international bestseller, garnering awards throughout the world, including a *Los Angeles Times* Book Award. Contemporary reviews of the novel were largely positive. Paul Gray, in a *Time* review, calls *The Unbearable Lightness of Being* "a triumph of wisdom over bitterness, hope over despair." Maureen Howard in the *Yale Review* writes, "*The Unbearable Lightness of Being* is the most rewarding new novel I've read in years." Thomas DePietro in *Commonweal* hones in on the heart of the book. He observes that *The Unbearable Lightness of Being* is a book of "burning compassion, extraordinary intelligence, and dazzling artistry." DePietro also notes the book "leaves us with many questions, questions about love and death, about love and transcendence. These are our burdens, the existential questions that never change but need to be asked anew."

Not all reviewers were enchanted with the book, however. Christopher Hawtree, in a *Spectator* review, faults Kundera for a "most off-putting" title and finds irksome the "elliptical structure" of the work. With faint praise, however, he acknowledges the novel is "a self-referential whole that manages not to alienate the reader." Wendy Lesser in the *Hudson Review* is even blunter, calling *The Unbearable Lightness of Being* "a bad novel." She particularly finds fault with Kundera's characterizations:

> The mistake Kundera makes is to treat his characters like pets. He thinks what he feels for them is love, whereas it's merely an excess of self. If it were really love, we would be able to push aside that gigantic authorial face that looms out of the pages of Kundera's novel … and find behind it the tiny, human, flawed faces of real novelistic characters. But they aren't there. Behind that leering, all-obliterating mask is nothing.

Scholarly interest in *The Unbearable Lightness of Being* continues unabated. Literary critics have found a variety of ways to read the novel. For example, John O'Brien in his book *Milan Kundera and Feminism* focuses on Kundera's representation of woman. He most notably studies the relationship between Tereza and Sabina, suggesting that Tereza represents "weight" and Sabina represents "lightness." O'Brien next demonstrates how Kundera undermines such an easy dichotomy. Finally, he argues that it is in Sabina's painting that Kundera reveals his true focal point.

In *Terminal Paradox*, scholar Maria Nemcová Banerjee takes another tact, reading the novel as if it were a piece of music. Just as Tereza introduces Tomas to Beethoven's quartets, and thus to the seminal phrase *Es muss sein*, Kundera introduces the reader to a quartet of characters: "The four leading characters perform their parts in concert, like instruments in a musical quartet, each playing his or her existential code in strict relation to those of the others, often spatially separated but never imaginatively isolated in the reader's mind."

Finally, Kamila Kinyon in *Critique* uses the French critical theory of Michel Foucault and the notion of the "panopticon" to analyze the book. Panopticon literally means "all-seeing," and it suggests a kind of surveillance mechanism. As Kinyon argues, "Within Kundera's novel, in a system of totalitarian Marxism where 'God is dead,' [the terrifying mystery] of God's gaze is replaced by [the terrifying mystery] of the panopticon camera, which may be directed at the individual at any time and which thus controls behavior even at those times when it is physically absent."

Sources

Banerjee, Maria Nemcová, *Terminal Paradox: The Novels of Milan Kundera*, Grove Press, 1990, p. 206.

Bayley, John, Review of *The Unbearable Lightness of Being*, in *London Review of Books*, Vol. 6, No. 10, June 7–20, 1984, pp. 18–19.

DePietro, Thomas, "Weighting for Kundera," in *Commonweal*, May 18, 1984, pp. 297–300.

Doctorow, E. L., Review of *The Unbearable Lightness of Being*, in *New York Times Book Review*, April 29, 1984, p. 1.

Gray, Paul, "Songs of Exile and Return," in *Time*, April 16, 1984, p. 77.

Hawtree, Christopher, "Bottom Rung," in *Spectator*, June 23, 1984, pp. 29–30.

Howard, Maureen, "Fiction in Review," in *Yale Review*, Vol. 74, No. 2, January 1985, pp. xxi–xxiii.

Kinyon, Kamila, "The Panopticon Gaze in Kundera's *The Unbearable Lightness of Being*," in *Critique*, Vol. 42, No. 3, Spring 2001, pp. 243–51.

Le Grand, Eva, *Kundera; or, the Memory of Desire*, translated by Lin Burman, Wilfred Laurier University Press, 1999, p. 3.

Lesser, Wendy, "The Character as Victim," in *Hudson Review*, Vol. XXXVII, No. 3, Autumn

1984, pp. 468–82.

O'Brien, John, *Milan Kundera and Feminism: Dangerous Intersections*, St. Martin's Press, 1995, p. 116.

Further Reading

Brink, André, *The Novel: Language and Narrative from Cervantes to Calvino*, New York University Press, 1998.

> Brink's book provides chapter-length analyses of a chronologically arranged series of novels. His chapter on *The Unbearable Lightness of Being* uses reader-response criticism to "explore the gaps."

Misurella, Fred, *Understanding Milan Kundera: Public Events, Private Affairs*, University of South Carolina Press, 1993.

> Misurella's book is an excellent, accessible starting point for the student wanting to further study Kundera.

Petro, Peter, ed., *Critical Essays on Milan Kundera*, G. K. Hall, 1999.

> This excellent collection of scholarly analyses and interviews with Kundera should prove valuable to those studying Kundera's work.

CPSIA information can be obtained
at www.ICGtesting.com
Printed in the USA
BVOW06s0241120917
494628BV00021B/191/P

9 781375 399210